Witness Lee

A Thorough View of the Body of Christ

Living Stream Ministry
Anaheim, CA • www.lsm.org

First Edition, May 1990.

ISBN 0-87083-512-2

Published by

Living Stream Ministry
2431 W. La Palma Ave., Anaheim, CA 92801 U.S.A.
P. O. Box 2121, Anaheim, CA 92814 U.S.A.

Printed in the United States of America

06   07   08   09   10   11   /   10   9   8   7   6   5   4   3

CONTENTS

PREFACE

This book contains translated messages released originally in Chinese by Brother Witness Lee during a conference at the Church in Taipei held on April 12 through April 15, 1990.

CHAPTER ONE

THE ORIGIN OF THE BODY OF CHRIST

Scripture Reading: Gal. 4:6; Rom. 8:15; John 1:12-13; 1 Pet. 1:2a; Luke 15:8, 17; John 16:8-11; 3:5-6; Rom. 8:19; 1 Cor. 6:15; 12:27; Col. 3:4a; 1 John 1:2; 5:11-12; John 3:36a; Matt. 28:19; 1 Cor. 12:13a; Col. 2:9; John 1:14a; Heb. 2:14a, 17-18; John 14:16-17; 7:39; Rev. 22:17a; 1 Cor. 15:3-4, 45b; John 15:1, 5; 17:21a, 23a

OUTLINE

I. God the Father being the believers' source—Gal. 4:6; Rom. 8:15:
   A. Who are begotten of God the Father—John 1:13.
   B. Who become the children of God the Father—John 1:12.
II. God the Spirit sanctifying and regenerating the ones selected and predestinated by God the Father:
   A. Sanctifying them—1 Pet. 1:2a:
      1. Enlightening and seeking them—Luke 15:8, 17.
      2. Convicting the enlightened ones—John 16:8-11.
   B. Regenerating them—John 3:5-6:
      1. To be the sons of God—Rom. 8:19.
      2. To be the members of Christ—1 Cor. 6:15; 12:27.
III. God the Son being life to the regenerated ones—Col. 3:4a:
   A. For the members of Christ to receive the uncreated and eternal life of God—1 John 1:2; 5:11-12; John 3:36a.
   B. Bringing the members of Christ into an organic union with the Triune God—Matt. 28:19.
IV. The Father, the Son, and the Spirit becoming the

consummated Spirit who baptizes the members of Christ into the unique Body of Christ—1 Cor. 12:13a:

A. The Father being embodied in the Son—Col. 2:9:
1. Passing through incarnation—John 1:14a; Heb. 2:14a.
2. Experiencing human life—Heb. 2:17-18.

B. The Son realized as the Spirit—John 14:16-17:
1. The Spirit being the consummated Spirit—John 7:39.
2. The Spirit being the ultimate consummation of the Triune God—Rev. 22:17a:
   a. Having passed through death and resurrection—1 Cor. 15:3-4.
   b. Becoming the all-inclusive, life-giving, indwelling, and compound Spirit—1 Cor. 15:45b.

C. Baptizing all the sanctified and regenerated ones into the Body of Christ—1 Cor. 12:13a:
1. Baptizing the regenerated ones into the Triune God—Matt. 28:19.
2. Making them one with the Triune God to be the Body of Christ—John 17:21a, 23a.

Prayer: Lord, we offer our worship to You. We thank You that You always take care of us and gather us, that You even gather us into Your holy name. Lord, we again gather into Your holy name tonight. May Your blood cleanse us, may Your Spirit be with us, and may Your Word be opened to us. Lord, we deeply believe that at this very moment You are present with us. You know that we are nothing and can do nothing. What we are looking to and depending on is You Yourself and Your blessing. Lord, lead us tonight, and guide every one of us. Do give each one of us a word which will touch the depths of our being, so that we would be supplied. Enlighten us that we may receive Your sustenance within. Lord, may You give us the utterance, the instant word, the fresh light. And we pray that You will release Yourself more and more so that we may be satisfied, and Your Body may be built up. Lord Jesus, grant us a clear sky. Through simple words reveal to us the mystery of Your Body. Grant us a thorough vision that we can see Your precious Body clearly. Be with us in an extraordinary way, and may Your all-pervading Spirit be upon us to touch us and possess us. Amen.

I have not been back here for a long time. I have come back, but this time I will not be staying too long, and after I leave, I will not return very soon. So I treasure these four meetings very much. I have had much consideration before the Lord and felt that I needed to speak some messages which are basic and crucial that will be sufficient for you for a year. If you know how to use them, they can even be adequate for your whole life.

A THOROUGH VIEW OF THE BODY OF CHRIST

The topic of the messages I am going to speak to you this time is "A Thorough View of the Body of Christ." I use the expression *thorough view* to talk about this matter because concerning the Body of Christ you have heard enough already. You all know that the Body of Christ is the church. This is not wrong, but this realization is too shallow. The Body is a mysterious matter. Not to mention the Body of Christ, just our little body is extremely mysterious; its mystery lies in its being organic. Look at me standing here. Because I am a living person, whether I am speaking or moving, regardless of what my body is doing, there is an organic expression. If our little physical bodies are like this, the Body of Christ is like this so much the more. Christ is the One who fills all in all (Eph. 1:23). He is such an immeasurable and boundlessly great Lord. He needs a Body of fullness to express Him even more than we do. From this you can realize how mysterious His Body is. It is not something that we can study thoroughly. Nevertheless, I am looking to the Lord that in these four days I may do my best to give you a thorough view of the Body of Christ.

In this first message tonight we will see the history of the Body of Christ, or the origin of the Body of Christ. Tomorrow in the second message we will see the elements, essence, and reality of the Body of Christ. In that message we will really be seeing a thorough view of the Body of Christ. In message three we will see the living in the Body of Christ. This is the living we ought to have. Of course, we do not live the life of a sinner, nor do we live the life of a natural person, nor do we merely live the life of a moral person or of an ordinary citizen; we live the Body life. When we talk about the church life, it is better to speak of the Body life. This word *church* has the denotation of a congregation, and a congregation, superficially speaking, does not have anything to do with life; but when the Body is mentioned, it clearly refers to a living organism. Finally, in the fourth message we will see the service of the Body of Christ. After we have seen the living in the Body, we will see the service of the Body.

THE ORIGIN OF THE BODY OF CHRIST

Now we must see the origin of the Body of Christ. We all know that everyone who is sitting here was born, not manufactured, into being. The idols in the temples are manufactured, not born. We human beings with our organic bodies are born into being from parents who are human beings like us. This birth is our origin. The Body of Christ is a totality of all the members of Christ, and we are the members in His Body. Therefore, in talking about the Body of Christ, we are all included, both you and I. When I speak about the Body of

Christ, I am speaking concerning you and also concerning myself. So when we talk about the origin of such a mysterious matter as Christ and His Body, you and I are both included. When we speak about the origin of the Body of Christ, we are speaking about our own origin.

God the Father Being the Believers' Source

The Body of Christ is similar to our human body; it was born into being, not manufactured. Its origin and source is the Triune God. And this Triune God has a name; He is called the Father, the Son, and the Spirit (Matt. 28:19). The Body of Christ came from Him, and He is our origin. According to the flesh, our source is our parents. Every one of us has a genealogy, a record of our origin. If we trace back our origin generation by generation, at the end the last generation is Adam. Regardless of our nationality or of our race, we all have a common source, that is, Adam. And Adam is from God; he was the son of God (Luke 3:38). Spiritually speaking, we who are the members of the Body of Christ came from the Triune God. The Triune God is the source of the Body of Christ.

The Triune God is the Father, the Son, and the Spirit. Yet these three—God the Father, God the Son, and God the Spirit—are one God. First, this Triune God is the Father, who is the source of us believers. Galatians 4:6 and Romans 8:15 show us that we who are regenerated and have a life union with God are the children of God; hence, we call God, "Abba Father." This God who has become our Abba Father is the source of you and me and is also the source of the Body of Christ. This Father God who has become our source has begotten us that we might become His children (John 1:12). Therefore, we have two births; one was our physical birth from our parents; the other was our spiritual birth from God our Father (1:13). According to the flesh, we are the children of our parents; hence, we have last names like Cheng, Lee, or Wang. But spiritually speaking, we were born of God the Father and are the children of God. Therefore, *God* becomes our common last name; our last name is God. God is our source. We are all the children of God, the members of the household of God (Eph. 2:19).

God the Spirit Sanctifying and Regenerating Those Whom God the Father Has Chosen and Predestinated

Sanctifying Them by Enlightening, Seeking, and Convicting Them

God the Father regenerated us in time, but in eternity past, long before the beginning of time and the creation of all things, He exercised His foreknowledge to select and predestinate us (Eph. 1:4-5), marking us out from among myriads of people. Then in time, at the right moment, God the Spirit, following the changes in the world situation and the environmental arrangement, sanctified us (1 Pet. 1:2a). This is what is recorded in Luke 15 concerning the Triune God saving sinners. There God the Spirit is likened to a woman lighting a lamp and sweeping the house to finely seek after the lost coin. Both you and I had this kind of experience when we were saved. While we listened to the gospel, the Holy Spirit was going along with the word of the gospel to enlighten and seek within us that we might be awakened (Luke 15:8, 17) and convicted concerning sin (John 16:8-11). Then we believed in our heart, confessed with our mouth, and called on the name of the Lord Jesus. Thus, we were saved and were regenerated to be the sons of God (Rom. 8:19), the members of the Body of Christ (1 Cor. 6:15; 12:27).

We became the members of the Body of Christ because the Holy Spirit, when we repented and believed in the Lord, entered into us so that we received the life of God and became regenerated. Actually, this Holy Spirit who has entered into us is the life of God becoming life within us. From that day on, there has been something additional within us. Sometimes this something within us rebukes and regulates us. This is not merely the functioning of our conscience. Rather, we have something more within us, the Lord who has become our living person. This is tremendous. My burden is to show you that the source of the Body of Christ is the Father; He is the source of life. Through His Spirit He has sanctified us and regenerated us that we might become the sons of God, the members of Christ. I hope that all of you sitting here will be clear concerning this matter. Today we do not believe into a religion, nor do we join a religion. We believe into a living and true Triune God. As soon as we repented and believed into Him, this Triune God as the Spirit came into us to be our life, to enliven us, and to make us a part of the organic Body of Christ. For this reason, many young people who believed in the Lord, though they were persecuted greatly and faced opposition from their parents, still stood firmly. Regardless of the situation, they still believe in the Lord, not because they are strong, but because they have a life within them that is strong. This life is the Triune God Himself; it includes God the Father, God the Son, and God the Spirit.

Regenerating Them to Become the Sons of God and the Members of Christ

Now that we have obtained this life, we are no longer individual persons, but members of the Body of Christ. Hence, we must not be disconnected from the Body. No member must be disconnected from the Body; once disconnected, the members are finished. Today every one of us is a member, a member of the Body of Christ. This Body of Christ is the church. Why do I say the Body and not the church? Because the church is a gathering, but the Body is an organism. A congregation can be dismissed, but a body cannot be disconnected. You may stop coming to the meetings, but you must not be disconnected from the Body. It may be possible sometimes to miss the meetings, but once the Body is disconnected, it is finished. But I can tell you that those who are in the meetings may not be in the Body, but those who are in the Body are definitely in the meetings. Those who do not come to the meetings are not necessarily disconnected from the Body, but those who are disconnected from the Body will definitely not come to the meetings. Therefore, being absent from the meetings may be somewhat risky; if you are not careful, you may soon be disconnected from the Body. Not coming to the meetings is close to being disconnected.

Let me repeat that the church is a kind of congregation, but the Body is a matter of life. All of us have life, but if we say that each one of us has been joined to the church, it is not so accurate. The real significance is that we have become the members of the Body of Christ, possessing the same one life and needing one another. This is to be members one of another. Therefore, whatever we do must be in the Body, joined to the Body, and regulated by the Body, because we are one Body. This is a wonderful matter.

God the Son Being Life
to the Regenerated Ones

We, the members of the Body of Christ, have God the Father as our source, God the Spirit as the One who sanctified and regenerated us, and God the Son as our life (Col. 3:4a). While it is true that we were regenerated by the Holy Spirit, according to the truth, it is God the Son who has become our life. Of course, the Triune God—the Father, the Son, and the Spirit—cannot be separated. If you have the Son, you have the Father; and if you have the Father, you have the Spirit. But according to the clear word and revelation of the Bible, when the Holy Spirit regenerated us, He brought Christ to us. This Christ becomes our life within so that we, the members of Christ, may have the uncreated, eternal life of God (1 John 1:2; 5:11-12; John 3:36a). At the same time, this life causes us to have an organic union with the Triune God so that we can enjoy all the riches of the Triune God (Matt. 28:19). This is like the union brought in by electric current. Our meeting hall and the power plant are joined together through the electric current. When the electric current comes to the meeting hall from the power plant, the meeting hall and the power plant are connected and joined together. Thus, the meeting hall receives all the benefits of the power plant, by which we enjoy air conditioning, lights, the sound system, and so on. Today's modern living depends especially on the union between the power plant and every place that electricity is applied. If this union is cut off, our life is also finished. Just imagine what it would be like if the electric current here suddenly stopped; we would all be in darkness.

Today within each one of the members of Christ, there is something which connects and joins him or her to the Triune God; this is the organic union of the life of God. We have all been regenerated, Christ has become our life within, and this life causes us to have a union with the Triune God. Therefore, now we are in the Triune God. The Triune God and we are connected together and joined together. All the riches of the Triune God become ours.

The Father, the Son, and the Spirit Becoming the Consummated Spirit Who Baptizes the Many Members of Christ into the Unique Body of Christ

We have already seen that the Father is the source, that the Spirit came to regenerate, and that the Son came to be life, so that we and the Triune God may have an organic union. This is the "inside" story of the members of the Body of Christ. There is also an "outside" story; that is, the Triune God—the Father, the Son, and the Spirit—having become the consummated Spirit, came to baptize the members of Christ into the unique Body of Christ (1 Cor. 12:13a). God's essence is Spirit, and the last person in His divine Trinity is also the Spirit. Not only so, the totality of the Father, the Son, and the Spirit eventually also became the consummated Spirit to baptize the members of Christ, those who have been regenerated by the Spirit and who have the Father as the source and the Son as the life, into one Body.

You and I have been saved. Through regeneration, we have the Spirit, Christ, and life within. Also, through the baptism of the Holy Spirit once outwardly, we all have been baptized into the Body. Inwardly, we were regenerated to have life; outwardly, the Spirit was poured upon us so that we might be baptized into one Body. This completes the origin of the Body.

Now we have to see how the Triune God became the ultimate and completed Spirit. First, the Father was embodied in the Son (Col. 2:9) through incarnation (John 1:14a; Heb. 2:14a). The Son experienced human life (Heb. 2:17-18), was crucified and resurrected, and was realized as the Spirit. Before the Son was realized as the Spirit, the Spirit was there already.

However, He was not yet completed. It was not until the Lord Jesus was resurrected from the dead and realized as the Spirit that the Spirit was completed (John 7:39). This completed Spirit is the ultimate completion of the Triune God (Rev. 22:17a), which implies that the Son through death and resurrection (1 Cor. 15:3-4) became the all-inclusive, life-giving, indwelling, and compound Spirit (1 Cor. 15:45b), to baptize all the sanctified, regenerated persons into the Triune God (Matt. 28:19), so that they and the Triune God could become one (John 17:21a, 23a) and be baptized into the Body of Christ (1 Cor. 12:13a).

Therefore, every time we preach the gospel and bring people to be saved, we baptize them into the name of the Father, the Son, and the Holy Spirit as soon as they confess the Lord's name. Their outward expression corresponds to an inward fact; that is, by being baptized into the Triune God, the saved ones and the Triune God have been made one. By their becoming one with the Triune God, they become members of the Body of Christ.

THE TRIUNE GOD BEING FULLY MINGLED WITH THE TRIPARTITE MAN

Finally, I must tell you the story of this Body of Christ. Simply speaking, it is the story of the Triune God mingling as one with us, the chosen and predestinated ones. Long before time began, in eternity past before all things were created, God by His eternal foreknowledge selected us and also marked us out. Then in time the Holy Spirit came to work, to seek us and regenerate us. This regeneration is the beginning of the mingling between the Triune God and us, and it is also the first step of the Triune God being life to us after coming into us. This happens in our spirit. From then on, if we cooperate with Him, love Him, and fellowship with Him, He will have the opportunity to spread outward from our spirit to our soul so that our mind can be renewed and transformed. This indwelling Spirit is like a dove, gradually and gently occupying and saturating us. He also will spread from our soul to our body to give life to our mortal bodies (Rom. 8:11). In this way, the Triune God and we, the tripartite men, will be completely mingled as one.

BEING FILLED WITH THE ESSENTIAL SPIRIT WITHIN AND RECEIVING THE OUTPOURING OF THE ECONOMICAL SPIRIT WITHOUT

At this point, we can clearly see that we have not only the Spirit within but also the Spirit without. This Spirit who has come upon us causes us to have the feeling of the Body. The Spirit inwardly is the Spirit of life; the Spirit outwardly is the Spirit of work. The inward Spirit of life is essential; the outward Spirit of work is economical. In actuality, these two are one Spirit. On the one hand, within us He is the essential Spirit; on the other hand, upon us He is the economical Spirit. Within us we have Him; outside of us we also have Him.

All the people along the lower Yangtze River in China like to drink tea in the morning to fill their stomachs with water. They say that this is wrapping water with skin. In the evening, they like to soak themselves in the bathtub; they say that this is wrapping skin with water. They wrap water with skin in the morning and skin with water in the evening. I feel that this is quite meaningful. If today all the Christians were like this, filled with the Spirit in the morning and receiving the outpouring of the Spirit in the evening, we would surely be members who are not disconnected but who are meeting and living in the Body. In the New Testament, there is a verse which speaks of the two sides of this matter. This is 1 Corinthians 12:13 which says, "For also in one Spirit we were all baptized into one body, whether Jews or Greeks, whether slaves or free, and were all given to drink one Spirit." To drink the Spirit is to wrap the "water" with "skin"; to be baptized into the one Body is to wrap "skin" with the "water." On the one hand, there is the Holy Spirit filling us within as the essential Spirit that we may have the life supply; on the other hand, there is the Holy Spirit poured out upon us outwardly as the economical Spirit to baptize us into the Body of Christ. Therefore, we may say that the origin of the Body of Christ is entirely a matter of the Spirit. There is the Spirit within, regenerating, transforming, and supplying us with life; this is the essential Spirit. There is also the Spirit without, being poured upon us; this is the economical Spirit.

All the problems taking place today in the church are due to neglecting the inner, essential Spirit for life as well as the outward, economical Spirit for work. Now since we have seen the origin of the Body of Christ and have also realized that everything related to the Body of Christ is entirely a matter of the Spirit, we should not pay attention to other things; we should only take care of the inward, essential Spirit for life and also the outward, economical Spirit for work that we may be normal and proper members in the Body of Christ. Hence, when we all follow the inward, essential Spirit for life and cooperate all the time with the outward, economical Spirit for work, and when we all live in the Body of Christ, we will be the organic Body of Christ. This is what we should see and what we should remain in.

(A message given by Brother Witness Lee on April 12, 1990, in Taipei, Taiwan.)

CHAPTER TWO

THE ELEMENTS, ESSENCE, AND REALITY OF THE BODY OF CHRIST

Scripture Reading: Eph. 4:4-6; John 20:22; Rom. 8:4, 6, 9-11, 13b; Gal. 2:20a; 1 Cor. 1:2a; John 3:5-6, 29; Titus 3:5; Rom. 12:2a; Eph. 4:23; 2 Cor. 3:18; Phil. 3:21; Rom. 8:30; John 17:21a, 23a; 1 Cor. 6:17; 1 Tim. 3:15b-16; John 15:1, 5; John 7:39; Rev. 22:17a; Phil. 1:19; 2 Cor. 4:16; Phil. 3:10a; John 14:17; 15:26; 16:13-15; 1 John 5:6; Rom. 15:16b; 14:17; Eph. 3:16; 1:23

OUTLINE

I. The elements of the Body of Christ:
   A. The processed Triune God—the divine element— Eph. 4:4-6:
      1. The Triune God passing through incarnation, crucifixion, and resurrection in order to enter into the members of Christ to be the element of the Body of Christ—John 20:22.
      2. The Triune God, having entered into the members of Christ, existing and living in the Body of Christ together with the members of Christ— Rom. 8:9-11; Gal. 2:20a.
   B. The tripartite man regenerated by God—the human element—1 Cor. 1:2a:
      1. Their spirit being regenerated—John 3:5-6; Titus 3:5.
      2. Their soul being renewed and transformed— Rom. 12:2a; Eph. 4:23; 2 Cor. 3:18.
      3. Their body being transfigured and glorified— Phil. 3:21; Rom. 8:30.

    C. The Triune God being mingled with the tripartite man—Eph. 4:4-6:

      1. The tripartite man becoming one with the Triune God—John 17:21a, 23a.

      2. The tripartite man becoming one spirit with the Triune God—1 Cor. 6:17.

    D. Issuing in a hybrid entity of divinity mingled with humanity:

      1. The Triune God, who possesses divinity with humanity, being mingled with the tripartite man, who possesses humanity with divinity—Rom. 8:6, 10-11.

      2. Divinity begotten in humanity, living in humanity, and expressed in humanity; humanity begotten of divinity, living by divinity, and expressing divinity—1 Tim. 3:15b-16.

      3. Issuing in an organism in which God is life to man and man has God as life—John 15:1, 5.

II. The essence of the Body of Christ:

    A. The Spirit as the essence of the Triune God becoming the essence of the Body of Christ—Eph. 4:4:

      1. The Spirit being the ultimate consummation of the processed Triune God—John 7:39; Rev. 22:17a.

      2. The Spirit bringing the processed Triune God into the Body of Christ through regeneration—John 3:5-6, 29; Eph. 4:5-6.

      3. The Spirit as the processed and consummated God, containing divinity and humanity, the all-inclusive death of Christ, and His surpassing resurrection, becoming not only the element of the Body, but also the essence of the Body—cf. Exo. 30:23-25.

    B. The capacities of the essence of the Body of Christ:

      1. The essence of the Body of Christ, containing the divinity of the Triune God, having the capacity to supply the divine life—Phil. 1:19.

      2. The essence of the Body of Christ, containing

the excelling humanity, having the capacity to supply the excelling humanity—2 Cor. 4:16.

3. The essence of the Body of Christ, containing the all-inclusive death of Christ, having the capacity to put to death the negative things—Rom. 8:13b.

4. The essence of the Body of Christ, containing the surpassing resurrection of Christ, having the surpassing capacity of resurrection—Phil. 3:10a.

III. The reality of the Body of Christ:

A. The reality of the processed Triune God being His consummated Spirit of reality—John 14:17; 15:26; 16:13; 1 John 5:6:

1. The reality of all that the Triune God is, has, and can do being this Spirit of reality.

2. The reality of the death and resurrection which the Triune God passed through also being this Spirit of reality.

B. This Spirit of reality making everything of the processed Triune God a reality in the Body of Christ—John 16:13-15:

1. All that the processed Triune God is, including righteousness, holiness, life, light, power, grace, and all the divine attributes, being realized by this Spirit of reality to be the attributes of the Body of Christ in reality—Rom. 15:16b; 14:17; Eph. 3:16.

2. All that the processed Triune God experienced, including incarnation, crucifixion, and resurrection, also being realized by this Spirit of reality to be the experiences of the Body of Christ in reality.

IV. The essence and reality of the Body of Christ being altogether matters of the Spirit of the processed and consummated Triune God:

A. This Spirit being the secret to all that the processed Triune God is to the Body of Christ:

1. The Spirit being the processed Triune God.

2. The Spirit being the totality of all the attributes of the processed Triune God.

3. The Spirit also being the effectiveness of all the processes of the processed Triune God.

B. This Spirit dwelling in our regenerated spirit, being joined as one spirit with our spirit—Rom. 8:9-11a; 1 Cor. 6:17:

1. We should have our whole being turned to and set on this joined spirit—Rom. 8:6b.

2. We should also live and walk according to this joined spirit—Rom. 8:4.

3. When we thus live in this joined spirit, we can live out the Body of Christ to become the corporate expression of Christ—Eph. 1:23.

Prayer: Lord, we worship You again from the depths of our being. How merciful You are to us. In Your mercy we are once again gathered into Your holy name to seek after You in Your Word. Lord, how profound Your Word is! We remind You that we need Your revelation, Your light, and, even more, Yourself, to unveil it to us. Lord, we really thank You that in this last age You have again and again opened Your holy Word to us and have brought us into the depths of Your Word. Tonight, Lord, we especially need You to open the understanding of our heart as well as our eyes, to speak to us and to release Your light, that we may really see the mysterious revelation in Your Word. Lord, may You gain the glory, may we receive the blessing, may the evil one get the shame, and may the church be built up. Amen.

CONCERNING ELEMENT, ESSENCE, AND REALITY

Tonight we come to the second message. This is a long and deep message concerning the elements, essence, and reality of the Body of Christ. First, we will consider three terms: *element, essence,* and *reality*. Element is a kind of constituent of a certain thing. Those who study chemistry know that chemistry is mainly the study of the constituents of matter, and the constituents are the elements. Even this podium has its constituent, which is mostly wood. The Body of Christ is something substantial yet mysterious in this universe. Though it is mysterious, it is nevertheless substantial. Therefore, the Body also has its constituents, and the constituents are its elements. Moreover, within every element or constituent there is a substance. Different constituents have different substances. For instance, steel has its own substance and wood has its own. This substance is what we call the essence.

For example, the main constituents of lemon tea are lemon, honey, water, and tea. These four constituents all possess different essences. In pharmaceutics, certain drugs are produced by extracting particular essences from herbs, which in turn give the drugs their special effects. Hence, the effectiveness of a drug depends on its essence. The church as the Body of Christ also has its own elements or constituents, within which are their essences and substance.

Let us consider the meaning of *reality*. According to the biblical usage of the word, *reality* refers to the real condition of men and things. For instance, we may hear of a church which is under much blessing, where all the saints love and fear the Lord, serve with zeal, love one another, and are holy and patient. When we go into their midst and truly witness such a situation among them, we may say that this particular church has much reality and that what we heard about them is real. In reading the Bible, we find that God is our love, light, life, power, righteousness, and holiness. We do not merely agree with this but also treasure His richness and all-inclusiveness. However, these riches are not merely printed words to us; they are both true and real. It is here that the greatest difference between the Bible and the writings of Confucius and Mencius lies. While the books of these men also discuss humility, forbearance, kindness, justice, courtesy, wisdom, and faithfulness, these are matters only in words and not in reality. The Bible, on the other hand, is different. When it says that God is holy, it is not merely words; there is such a reality. We are not required to work out a kind of holiness; rather, it is the holy God Himself who works holiness into our being through His Spirit. In this way, God's holiness becomes our reality. Whatever the Bible says becomes reality in us if we receive it from God.

The Bible says that God Himself is reality (John 1:14-17). If there is holiness, He is holiness; if there is light, He is light; if there is life, He is life; and if there is patience, He is patience. If we believe and receive Him, we will gain the reality of all that He is. If we have only the printed words of the Bible, we possess mere teachings and doctrines without reality. However, we have not only the Word of God but also the Spirit of God. The Spirit of God accompanies the Word of God to work into us as reality what the Bible utters.

MAN WITHOUT AND GOD WITHIN

Now that we have acquired a clear impression concerning element, essence, and reality, we can apply all three to the Body of Christ. Since the church is the Body of Christ, it must possess its own constituents and elements. The blood, the cells, the skin, the flesh, and the bones are all constituents of the human body, and these in turn have their own essences and substances. What then are the essences and constituents in the Body of Christ? Two essences constitute the Body of Christ. One is the processed Triune God, which is the divine element; the other is the tripartite man regenerated by God, which is the human element. These two elements are two constituents. The constituent of the processed Triune God enters into us to mingle with us, the tripartite man, to produce the Body of Christ. When we were saved and regenerated, God in Christ came into us to be the divine life in us, and this divine life became the divine essence within us.

However, merely to have Christ as the essence of the divine life within us does not result in the church, since the church is the mingling of divinity with humanity, that is, man without and God within. We realize that although the church and a social club are both human gatherings, there is a great difference between them. A club is an association of people who share certain traits, such as a common birthplace. The church is different; it has people from all places. What we have in common is not our birthplace, but God. You have God in you; I have God in me; he has God in him—we all have God in us. Whenever God is mentioned, everyone responds. This is the "God-responsiveness" in us. Hence, the church is different from any kind of group, such as professional societies and trade unions. In these associations, there are only human beings without God in them. The church, however, is not only men; there is God within. That which has only men and not God is not the church. A single constituent is not enough; there must be both the divine constituent as well as the human constituent. We can say that the church is both man and God. It is the mingling of God and man, the blending of humanity with divinity, a hybrid entity of divinity joined with humanity, with two elements or constituents.

Not only so, within the two elements of the Body of Christ are the essences and substances of each. Thus, besides having the human element with its human essence, the church also possesses the divine element with its divine essence. Human organizations frequently have friction and disputes due to self-interest and self-gain. This is because among them there is only the human essence and not the divine essence. In the church of God there is not only the human essence but also the divine essence. There is no room for man's natural flesh. On the contrary, since we all have the element of God's life with the divine essence within us, the church displays an uncommon condition, one which expresses the reality of God.

THE ELEMENTS OF THE BODY OF CHRIST

The Processed Triune God—
the Divine Element

Now we will follow the outline to get into this present message, which is entitled "The Elements, Essence, and Reality of the Body of Christ." Let us start with the elements of the Body of Christ. The first item is the processed Triune God, who is the divine element (Eph. 4:4-6). The church is different from all organizations because it possesses the divine element of the processed Triune God. This Triune God passed through incarnation, crucifixion, and resurrection in order to enter into the members of Christ that they might be the elements of the Body of Christ (John 20:22).

God is holy, righteous, and glorious. In order to enter into us, the filthy sinners, He first became flesh and put on a body of flesh and blood that He might be crucified for us and shed His blood to make propitiation for our sins and satisfy the righteous requirement of God's law. He also resurrected to become the life-giving Spirit so that He might get into all who believe in Him and call upon Him. When we obtain Him in this way, He becomes our life element and life constituent within us.

Now this Triune God who has entered into us, the members of Christ, has not only become our life element and constituent, but also exists together, lives together, and mingles with us who are the members of the Body of Christ (Rom. 8:9-11; Gal. 2:20a). Some of us did have these experiences. Before we were saved and had the divine life and divine constituent in us, we frequently quarreled with our spouse. Such arguments were usually intensified and strengthened by reasonings as they went on. After we believed in the Lord Jesus and the divine element of the Triune God entered into us, He often stopped us just when we were about to start an argument. This is because the Lord Jesus, in whom we have believed, came into us to be our divine element. Whereas once we were a cup full of bitter water, now the bitterness is diminishing and the water is being sweetened by the addition of the "lemon" and "honey."

The Tripartite Man Regenerated by God—
the Human Element

The second item of the elements of the Body of Christ is the tripartite man regenerated by God as the human element (1 Cor. 1:2a). Each one of us who was saved and belongs to the Body of Christ possesses these two elements or constituents, that is, the divine constituent and the human constituent. Moreover, we human beings regenerated by God have three parts: the spirit, the soul, and the body. First, God comes into our spirit to regenerate it (John 3:5-6; Titus 3:5); then, He spreads into our soul that it may be renewed and transformed (Rom. 12:2a; Eph. 4:23; 2 Cor. 3:18); and finally, He saturates our body that it may be transfigured and glorified (Phil. 3:21; Rom. 8:30). Thus, our tripartite being and the Triune God are fully mingled as one (Eph. 4:4-6). The processed Triune God is the divine constituent, and the tripartite being who has been possessed by God is the human constituent. When these two constituents are mingled, they become the constituents of the Body of Christ.

The Triune God Being Mingled with
the Tripartite Man to Become a Hybrid Entity

The mingling of the divine element of the Triune God and the human element of the tripartite man can be likened to the blending of lemon and honey with water to make lemonade. The issue of the Triune God entering into and mingling with us, the tripartite man, is that we become one with the Triune God (John 17:21a, 23a) and are one spirit with the Triune God (1 Cor. 6:17) as a hybrid entity of divinity and humanity blended together. Every saved person is a hybrid of divinity and humanity mingled together. The dual nature of this hybrid is the divine with the human. Though we are human beings, we have God within us. Since God and man have become one entity, we are the God-men. This hybrid entity of God mingled with man is just the Triune God, who possesses divinity with humanity, mingled with the tripartite man, who possesses humanity with divinity (Rom. 8:6, 10-11). Because our God passed through incarnation, He possesses divinity with humanity; and because God entered into us at the time of our salvation and regeneration, we possess humanity with divinity. Whether it is divinity with humanity or humanity with divinity, both include the dual nature of God and man and thus result in a hybrid of divinity and humanity.

Further, the hybrid issuing from the mingling of divinity with humanity is a matter of divinity being begotten in humanity, living in humanity, and being expressed in humanity; it is also a matter of humanity being begotten by divinity, living by divinity, and expressing divinity (1 Tim. 3:15b-16). Divinity being begotten in humanity, living in humanity, and being expressed in humanity refers to the Lord Jesus as God incarnate. Humanity being begotten by divinity, living by divinity, and expressing divinity points to the Body of Christ, which is constituted by persons who have been regenerated by God. This hybrid of the mingling of God and man eventually becomes an organism in which God is life to man and man has God as life (John 15:1, 5). This is the church, the Body of Christ.

THE ESSENCE OF THE BODY OF CHRIST

The Spirit Being the Essence of the Triune God

Let us now continue with the second major point, the essence of the Body of Christ. The Spirit as the essence of the Triune God has become the essence of the Body of Christ (Eph. 4:4). Hence, the essence of the Body of Christ is the Spirit, who is the consummation of the processed Triune God (John 7:39; Rev. 22:17a). The Triune God—the Father, the Son, and the Spirit—are all in this all-inclusive and consummated Spirit. Further, the Spirit, through regeneration, has brought the processed Triune God into the Body of Christ, that is, into us the regenerated persons (John 3:5-6, 29; Eph. 4:5-6). Besides this, the Spirit as the processed and consummated God, containing divinity and humanity, the all-inclusive death of Christ, and His surpassing resurrection, became not only the element of the Body of Christ but also its essence (cf. Exo. 30:23-25). Both the element and essence of the Body of Christ are this all-inclusive Spirit, who is the ultimate consummation of the Triune God. The Spirit, who is in the Body of Christ, is the Body's element on the one hand and its essence on the other hand. This may be likened to the addition of the constituent and element of lemon to water by adding lemon juice into water. Such a particular constituent and element contain an essence, which may be called lemon extract. This essence of lemon extract comes from the constituent and element of the lemon.

The Capacities of the Essence of the Body of Christ

The Spirit as the essence of the Triune God has now become the essence of the Body of Christ, and there are certain precious capacities associated with this essence. Each essence has its own capacities. For instance, a lemon has the constituent and element of lemon, and within that constituent and element is an essence called lemon extract. This lemon extract possesses a capacity to soothe our throats. Another example is the various types of antibiotics with their different constituents and element and thus their different essences. Each essence brings about a different capacity to cure a different disease.

The Spirit, who is the essence of the Triune God as well as the consummated Triune God Himself, became not only the element but also the essence of the Body of Christ. Such an essence also possesses its own capacities. First, the essence of the Body of Christ contains the divinity of the Triune God with the capacity to supply the divine life (Phil. 1:19). The Spirit as the essence of the Triune God becoming the essence of the Body of Christ is able to supply God's life and nature into us. This is His capacity. Second, the essence of the Body of Christ contains the excelling humanity with the capacity to supply the same excelling humanity to us (2 Cor. 4:16). The humanity of the Lord Jesus is high and excelling. He possesses not only a rich divinity but also a surpassing humanity. We can clearly see this in the Gospels' record of His feeding the crowd with five loaves and two fishes (Matt. 14:14-21). A great crowd gathered in the wilderness one evening and had nothing to eat. After the Lord received the five loaves and two fishes from the disciples, He ordered the people to sit down in rows. Then He looked up to heaven, blessed and broke the food, and gave it to the people. After the crowd ate and was full, He charged the disciples to gather the leftovers, which eventually filled twelve baskets. Here we can see that while the Lord richly supplied the people in His rich divinity, He did not waste anything but cherished what God had blessed. What a high and excelling humanity this is! When we were saved, the Lord Jesus not only delivered us from sin; He also entered into us to be our life and to supply us with His excelling humanity in order that our own humanity may be transformed and uplifted.

Third, the essence of the Body of Christ contains the all-inclusive death of Christ, with the capacity to put to death the negative things (Rom. 8:13b). Just as antibiotics possess germ-killing essences, the all-inclusive death of Christ is able to kill all the negative things in us. The redemption accomplished by Christ through His cross two thousand years ago can now be applied to us through His eternal Spirit. The effectiveness of His death is operative in us because the Spirit of His essence contains the all-inclusive death of Christ, and this Spirit is now in us. When He operates in us, this Spirit contains the capacity to kill all the negative things and will put to death all the negative "germs" in us, much like antibiotics.

Fourth, the essence of the Body of Christ also contains the surpassing resurrection of Christ with the surpassing capacity of resurrection (Phil. 3:10a). Although we often feel sorrowful and depressed in our Christian life, whenever we look to the Lord and fellowship with Him, there is a kind of inner surpassing power which simply carries us through our situations. Such surpassing power is the resurrection of Christ in us becoming our surpassing essence. The resurrection of Christ raised Him from Hades, and He ascended into the heavens to be far above all. Now this surpassing resurrection in the Spirit, who has become the essence of the Body of Christ, enables us to participate in its capacity in the same Body.

THE REALITY OF THE BODY OF CHRIST

The Spirit of the Reality of the Triune God

The third major point concerns the reality of the Body of Christ. We have already indicated that reality refers to the real condition of persons and things. The Body of Christ is the church today, and all of its reality is the Spirit of the reality of the consummated Triune God. The reality of the processed Triune God is His consummated Spirit of reality (John 14:17; 15:26; 16:13; 1 John 5:6). The reality of all that the Triune God is, has, and can do is simply this Spirit of reality. The reality of the death and resurrection which the Triune God passed through is also this Spirit of reality.

Furthermore, this Spirit of reality makes everything of the processed Triune God a reality in the Body of Christ (John 16:13-15). It is this same Spirit of reality who makes all the riches of the Triune God, which are just His reality, possible and real in the Body of Christ. All that the processed Triune God is, including righteousness, holiness, life, light, power, grace, and all the divine attributes, are realized by this Spirit of reality to be the real attributes of the Body of Christ (Rom. 15:16b; 14:17; Eph. 3:16). Originally, such righteousness, holiness, life, light, power, and grace were merely God's attributes; now these attributes have been realized in the church by the Spirit in the Body of Christ. The church therefore possesses the reality of the divine attributes, such as righteousness, holiness, life, light, power, and grace.

Furthermore, all that the Triune God experienced, including incarnation, crucifixion, and resurrection, are likewise realized by this Spirit of reality to be the real experiences of the Body of Christ. Originally, it was the Triune God who was incarnated, crucified, and resurrected. But when the Spirit of reality came, He made these experiences of the Triune God real in us as our real experiences. Because of this we can live a normal human life on the earth today. We can deal with the negative matters which befall us by the capacity of the death of Christ. We do not lose our temper, nor do we blame or rebuke others, because the death of Christ is realized in us through the Spirit of reality. Moreover, the Spirit with the resurrection of Christ works in us to enable us to love and forgive others. These are all examples of how the experiences of the Triune God Himself have been realized in the church by the Spirit of reality to be the real experiences of the church. This is the Spirit of the reality of the Triune God becoming the reality of the Body of Christ.

THE ESSENCE AND REALITY OF THE BODY OF CHRIST BEING ALTOGETHER MATTERS OF THE SPIRIT OF THE PROCESSED AND CONSUMMATED TRIUNE GOD

Finally, we need to see conclusively that both the essence and the reality of the Body of Christ are altogether matters of the Spirit of the processed and consummated Triune God. Whether essence or reality, it is all a matter of this Spirit. The Spirit is the reality of the essence as well as the essence to which the reality belongs. *Essence* emphasizes the inward substance, while *reality* emphasizes the outward realization. Because the Spirit is the inward substance of the Body of Christ, He is also its outward realization. Both the inward essence and substance and the outward reality and realization are of the Spirit. This Spirit is the secret to all that the Triune God is to the Body of Christ. For instance, the secret to God's loving the Body of Christ, sanctifying it, and strengthening it, is with the Spirit of reality. It is the Spirit of reality who makes God's love real in the Body of Christ, so that it may be sanctified and strengthened. This Spirit of reality is the processed Triune God Himself as well as the totality of all the attributes of the processed Triune God. If we have this Spirit, we have all the attributes of the processed Triune God, such as love, light, mercy, righteousness, holiness, life, power, and grace. Furthermore, the Spirit is also the effectiveness of all the processes of the processed Triune God. Incarnation, crucifixion, and resurrection all have their effectiveness, and their effectiveness is just the Spirit of essence and reality. The effectiveness of both the death and resurrection of Christ is displayed in us who possess this Spirit of essence and reality.

OUR WHOLE PERSON BEING TURNED TO AND SET ON THE JOINED SPIRIT AND LIVING ACCORDING TO IT

This Spirit now dwells in our regenerated Spirit and is joined to our spirit as one spirit (Rom. 8:9-11a; 1 Cor. 6:17). He is not only in us but also joined with our spirit to become one spirit with us. We must therefore exercise to turn our whole being to this joined spirit and set our mind on it (Rom. 8:6b). Do not place your mind on frivolous matters; set it on the spirit by turning your entire being to this joined spirit. We should also live and walk according to this joined spirit (Rom. 8:4). We must speak, do things, treat others, and deal with matters according to this joined spirit. We should talk to our family members in our home life according to this spirit. When we live in this joined spirit, we will be able to live out the Body of Christ and become His corporate expression (Eph. 1:23).

(A message given by Brother Witness Lee on April 13, 1990, in Taipei, Taiwan.)

CHAPTER THREE

THE LIVING IN THE BODY OF CHRIST

Scripture Reading: Eph. 5:23; Col. 3:4a, 11b; 1 Cor. 12:12; Eph. 1:23; Phil. 3:14; Eph. 4:4a; 1 John 5:6; Phil. 4:12b; Rom. 15:13; 6:6; 8:13b; Gal. 5:24; Eph. 2:6a; Phil. 3:10a; 1 John 5:11-12; Rom. 9:11b; Gal. 2:16a; Phil. 1:19-21a; Rom. 12:5

OUTLINE

I. Taking Christ as its Head, life, content, principal object, center, and goal:
  A. As its Head, life, and content—Eph. 5:23; Col. 3:4a, 11b:
    1. Concerning Christ as the source and element of His Body.
    2. Referring to the origin and being of the Body of Christ.
  B. As its principal object, center, and goal—1 Cor. 12:12; Eph. 1:23; Phil. 3:14:
    1. Concerning Christ as the meaning and expression of His Body.
    2. Referring to the capacity and function of the Body of Christ.
II. Having the Spirit as its essence and reality, and taking the Spirit as its secret and effectiveness:
  A. As its essence and reality—Eph. 4:4a; 1 John 5:6:
    1. Concerning the inward nature and the real outward state of the Body of Christ.
    2. Referring to the inward being and the outward manifestation of the Body of Christ.
  B. As its secret and effectiveness—Phil. 4:12b; Rom. 15:13:

      1. Concerning the skill and ability of the Body of Christ.

      2. Referring to the skillfulness and achievements of the Body of Christ.

III. Taking the crucifixion and resurrection of Christ as its regulation:

  A. Being regulated in the negative aspect by the crucifixion of Christ:

      1. Our crucifixion with Christ being an accomplished fact—realized through divine revelation— Rom. 6:6.

      2. Our crucifixion with Christ being the day-to-day experience that we that should have—enjoyed through the effectiveness of the Spirit—Rom. 8:13b; Gal. 5:24.

  B. Being regulated in the positive aspect by the resurrection of Christ:

      1. Our resurrection with Christ being an accomplished fact—Eph. 2:6a.

      2. Our resurrection with Christ being the day-to-day experience that we should have— Phil. 3:10a.

IV. Taking life and the Body as the principle:

  A. Taking life as the principle:

      1. Taking the inward life of God, which is just Christ as the embodiment of God, as the principle—1 John 5:11-12.

      2. Not taking the outward conduct and morality of man as the principle—Rom. 9:11b; Gal. 2:16a.

  B. Taking the Body as the principle:

      1. Every member living Christ out by the Spirit of life—Phil. 1:19-21a.

      2. Living corporately and coordinating to live out the Body of Christ to be the fullness of Christ to express Him—Rom. 12:5; Eph. 1:23.

In the last message, we saw the elements, essence, and reality of the Body of Christ. Now based on that, we are going to speak about the living of the Body of Christ. We all know that the living of human beings, birds, beasts, or cattle is according to the element and essence of its life. Birds fly in the air because they have the essence and capacity of flying. Cats catch mice and dogs bark because they each have their respective essence and capacity.

THE TRIUNE GOD AND THE BODY OF CHRIST

Ephesians 4:4 through 6 may be considered the most profound verses in the entire Bible. They say, "One Body and one Spirit, as also you were called in one hope of your calling; one Lord, one faith, one baptism; one God and Father of all, who is over all and through all and in all." Here there are seven "ones," which are divided into three groups. The first three items, one Body, one Spirit, and one hope, form the first group. The second three items, one Lord, one faith, and one baptism, form the second group. Lastly, one God and Father of all is the third group. Although these three verses are short, they are very mysterious, revealing to us that the Triune God—the Father, the Son, and the Spirit—is related to the Body of Christ.

One Body, One Spirit, and One Hope

These verses first mention "one Body"; this is then followed by the "one Spirit." This Spirit is the essence and reality of the Body of Christ. The essence is contained within and the reality is expressed without. The Spirit of the Triune God is the essence within the Body of Christ and the reality manifested without. This causes the Body to have a hope, which is regeneration and saturation by the Spirit unto the manifestation of the glory of God. This glory is our hope in the future (Col. 1:27). Every saved person has been born of the Spirit and has obtained the Spirit, who is the essence and reality of the Body of Christ. This Spirit wants to saturate us within continuously, to completely saturate our tripartite being so that we would eventually manifest the glory of divinity.

The worldly people live in this world without hope and

without God. When they are young, they desire to get into good schools; after graduation, they desire to go abroad to study, and then get a good job, find a good mate, have a family and business, and raise children. But eventually they still cannot escape becoming old, suffering illnesses, and finally dying. Then all their hopes are over. However, we are not like this. We have a glorious hope because within us we have the Spirit, who is the essence and reality of the Triune God, saturating us continuously. When the Lord comes back, He will be manifested from within us to bring us together with Him into glory.

One Lord, One Faith, and One Baptism

Beside this, there is also one Lord, that is, the Son in the divine Trinity. He came to be our life. This life became our element within, that is, the element of the Body of Christ. The Spirit is the essence of this Body as something within; He is also the reality of this Body as something without. The Lord is the element of this Body. Furthermore, there are also "one faith, one baptism." Originally we were all in Adam; our element was the element of Adam, the element of death, not the element of life. We were all dead in Adam. Strictly speaking, in Adam people are not living daily, but dying daily. A man's age is like savings in the bank. In the beginning you make a deposit, and then you continue to write checks. Your savings gradually decrease, and eventually there is nothing left and it is finished. When human beings live one day, they lose one day; when they live one year, they lose one year. This is the situation in Adam, where Adam is taken as the element. But when we believed in the Lord and were baptized into water, our old man was buried and the element which came from Adam was terminated. The Israelites crossing the Red Sea is a type of baptism. Once they crossed the Red Sea, their relationship with Egypt was severed. Similarly, through baptism we were severed from the element of Adam. Therefore, baptism is a termination, a severance; believing is an entering in and a joining. When we believed and were baptized, we came out of Adam; at the same time, we entered into Christ and were united to Christ. Hence, within us we have another life, which is a new life, a new element. The old life is the life of Adam, the element of Adam; the new one is Christ as life, Christ as the element. From this element of Christ comes the essence and reality of the Spirit. This implies that from Christ as the element of the Body of Christ comes the Spirit as the essence and reality of the Body of Christ.

We have said that the church is different from any human association. The church has God; an association does not have God. Hence, this church which has God becomes a Body, an organism, of Christ. Because a human association does not have life as the element, it will never become an organism. However, if there is no element of Christ in the church, but only the element of Adam, it is still not the organic Body of Christ. Although we have already been baptized, there is still the possibility that we remain in Adam and have Adam as the element, instead of the element of Christ. This then is not the church. Therefore, we must accept the dealing of the cross to deal with our old man and naturalness; we should let Adam go and let Christ come out. We are living a human life, yet we speak by Christ and even speak the word of Christ. When everyone is like this, we are the genuine church, because it is Christ who is the life and element here.

One God and Father of All

We have already been baptized, have come out of Adam and believed into Christ, and have been joined to Christ; hence, Christ is our life, our element; He is our Lord. Our Lord is our life. Therefore, these verses speak of one Body, one Spirit, and also one Lord. Finally, in addition, there is the one God and Father of all. Everything has its source. The source of the Body of Christ is the Father. Ephesians 4 does not only say one God, but one God and Father. This Father is the source, the source of the Body of Christ. The Lord is the element of the Body of Christ; the Spirit is the essence and reality of the Body of Christ; and the Father is the source of the Body of Christ. This Father is not only over all, through all, but also in all. He is one, yet He can be in three places at the same time—above, in the midst, and within. This is mingling. He is not only above us, but also through us, and even within us. This is the Triune God—the Father, the Son, and the Spirit.

THE FOUR ASPECTS OF THE RELATIONSHIP IN THE LIVING IN THE BODY OF CHRIST

Now we need to see the living in the Body of Christ. This living has four aspects in its relationship. The first aspect is the relationship with Christ. The living in the Body of Christ has Christ as the Head, life, content, principal object, center, and goal, because Christ is the element of this Body. The second aspect is the relationship with the Spirit. The living in the Body of Christ has the Spirit as the essence, reality, secret, and effectiveness, because the Spirit is the inward essence and the expressed reality of this Body. The third aspect is the relationship with the death and resurrection of Christ. The living in the Body of Christ takes the death and resurrection of Christ as the regulation. Every organism has its regulation, which cannot be violated. If we would live the life of the Body of Christ, we need to be in resurrection by the Spirit and through the cross. The fourth aspect is the relationship with life and the Body. Life and the Body are taken as the principle. The principle of the living in the Body of Christ is life, not behavior; and it is corporate, not individualistic. The combination of all these four aspects of relationship is the living in the Body of Christ, the Christian life, and also the church life.

Therefore, we see here that the living in the Body of Christ has four aspects to its relationship: Christ as the element, the Spirit as the essence, the death and resurrection as the regulation, and life and the Body as the principle. I can testify to you that I am alive until today because of the grace of God and also because I kept the regulation and principle of the body; hence, my body is still healthy. There is a lot to this matter. The living in the Body of Christ has its basic element, intrinsic essence, extrinsic reality, and also its regulation and principle. We live not only by the element, essence, and reality in this Body, but also within the regulation and principle of this living, being ruled and controlled by it.

THE LIVING IN THE BODY OF CHRIST

Taking Christ as Its Head, Life, Content, Principal Object, Center, and Goal

The first aspect in the relationship of the Body of Christ is its relationship with Christ. Christ is the center of the Triune God. Among the persons of the Triune God—the Father, the Son, and the Spirit—He is also the center. The Body of this Christ, who is the center of the Triune God, surely takes Him as its Head. We are all under the authority of Christ as the Head; He is our Head, our life. The living of the Body of Christ takes Christ as the Head, life, and content (Eph. 5:23; Col. 3:4a, 11b); this concerns Christ as the source and element of His Body and refers to the origin and being of the Body of Christ. Moreover, this living takes Christ as the principal object, the center, and the goal (1 Cor. 12:12; Eph. 1:23; Phil. 3:14). This concerns Christ as the meaning and expression of His Body and refers to the capacity and function of the Body of Christ. This shows that the Body of Christ is meaningful and active.

If an endeavoring person takes himself as the principal object and center, eventually he will hurt others. But if one is endeavoring yet does not center on himself, but on the goal of his endeavoring, he will benefit society and the country. All of us were made for God. If we, after getting saved, are not for God, but for ourselves, we are really pitiful and without hope. Therefore, for us Christians, our Head is Christ, our content is Christ, our principal object and center are also Christ, and even our goal is Christ. Because the nature of the Body of Christ is Christ, this causes its capacity also to be Christ. Today in the church, all of us are members of the Body of Christ. This Body of Christ has a principal object, a center, and a goal, which is Christ Himself. Because Christ is the principal object, the center, and the goal of the Body of Christ, we the members should also take Christ as our principal object, our center, and our goal. In this way we can give Him the opportunity to manifest the capacity and function within His nature. This is the church life that we have.

Taking the Spirit as Its Essence, Reality, Secret, and Effectiveness

The second aspect in the relationship of the Body of Christ is its relationship with the Spirit as its essence, reality, secret, and effectiveness. The essence and the reality (Eph. 4:4a; 1 John 5:6) are related to the intrinsic nature and the outward condition of the Body of Christ. They refer to the intrinsic being and the outward manifestation of the Body of Christ. Every matter has an intrinsic nature and an outward reality. There is an essence within us Christians, and the reality we manifest without should be the living out of this essence. Our essence is the Spirit, and the reality we live out should also be the Spirit. If we are not like this, we are "low-grade" Christians, lacking the intrinsic essence and the outward condition.

Since our intrinsic essence and outward reality are the Spirit, who is the pneumatic Christ, we should have fellowship with Him, allowing Him to fill us and saturate us. He is within us as our essence, saturating us so that there is the manifestation without as the reality of our Christian life. This then is the intrinsic being and the outward manifestation of the Body of Christ, the church. In this age today, what human society needs is a lamp which shines brightly. The Body of Christ, the church, filled with the Spirit within and manifesting the reality of Christ without, can shine this light to illuminate this dark age. The Lord Jesus said that we who belong to Him are the light of the world (Matt. 5:14). We are able to illuminate those who are in darkness. We cannot be like general Christianity, having just a name yet not the substance. We need to be filled with the Spirit within so that we can live Christ out.

The living of the Body of Christ also takes the Spirit as its secret and its effectiveness (Phil. 4:12b; Rom. 15:13). The Spirit, who is our inward essence and outward reality, is also the secret and effectiveness of our practice of the Body life. This concerns the skill and ability of the Body of Christ and refers to the skillfulness and achievements of the Body of Christ. We should not think that it is merely in our work that we need superior skill and capabilities; even in living the life of the Body of Christ, we also need technique and skills. Sometimes due to our lack of skill in speaking, we offend a lot of people and ruin matters. This is due to our lack of technique and skill in speaking. It is not simple to be a Christian. Before we were saved, we took our own way; after we are saved, we are bound together with Christ. Our living is like a three-legged race. We are regulated and restricted by Him in every aspect. If we are not wise and are short of technique and skill in our living, we will feel awkward and clumsy. But if we have the Spirit as the secret, knowing how to follow Christ, we will become happy and comfortable.

Immediately after some couples get married, during their honeymoon, they are sweet to one another. But after a few days, the real situation is exposed and they get into an argument. At that time they need to learn about each other and pick up some skill in conversing with each other in their daily living so that they may know how to speak, how to express themselves, and even how to be upset. Some get divorced simply because they do not have the skill to conduct themselves and they do not know the technique of being a human being. We who have God have the Spirit within us, who is our technique. Sometimes situations may arise in a home. If we are in our spirit, we would know how to speak and how to handle the situations; and in most cases, this could calm the wind and the waves. It is the same in the church life. Many times some things are not necessary. The unnecessary arguments and friction are due to our lack of the Spirit as the secret; there is no tactfulness nor refined skill in our living. This phrase *refined skill* implies beauty. Our living needs refined skill in order to be beautiful. If our behavior has this refined skill, our living will be full of merit.

If we can take the Spirit as the secret of our living, our behavior will be skillful, and we will not have arguments or discord. Our living will surely be full of merit. Therefore, in the living in the Body of Christ, in our speaking and in coping with situations, we need to have much prayer, receive more of the Spirit, allow more of the cross of Christ to break us, and live more by the resurrection of Christ. By doing this, our living in the Body of Christ will be full of skill and merit.

Taking the Crucifixion and Resurrection of Christ as Its Regulation

For this reason, in the living of the Body of Christ we need to take the crucifixion and resurrection of Christ as the regulation. On the negative side, we take the crucifixion of Christ as the regulation; on the positive side, we take the resurrection of Christ as the regulation. When we speak, we need to accept the dealing and regulation of the cross of Christ. Through this regulation, we will know how we should speak and what should be spoken or not spoken. Besides accepting the regulation of the crucifixion of Christ, we still need to know the resurrection of Christ and take the resurrection of Christ as the positive regulation. Christ who lives within us is not quiet and inactive; He is active and purposeful within us. He is not acting within us in a vigorous way, but is operating quietly yet powerfully within us. His operation is the power of His resurrection. If we go along with His operation, His resurrection power will come and cause us to be transcendent and victorious.

Today people are in a situation of bondage, living a life of oppression every day. Hence, we need the resurrection power, and Christ within us is this resurrection power. If we go along with Him, we can transcend all the circumstances and will not be under any oppression. On the one hand, through the crucifixion of the cross, we filter out everything that the Lord is not pleased with; on the other hand, we enjoy the transcendence of the resurrection of Christ. In Philippians 3:10 Paul says, "To know Him and the power of His resurrection...being conformed to His death." Paul was asking and praying in this way, so we should also ask and pray in this way so that we will not be under the oppression of any of our circumstances; rather, we can transcend and carry out the living of the Body of Christ.

Our co-crucifixion with Christ is an accomplished fact; this is realized through divine revelation (Rom. 6:6). Our co-crucifixion with Christ should also be our moment-by-moment experience; this is enjoyed through the effectiveness of the Spirit (Rom. 8:13b; Gal. 5:24). *Hymns,* #631 says, "If I'd know Christ's risen power, / I must ever love the cross; / Life from death alone arises; / There's no gain except by loss." We should have this prayer daily so that we may have this experience every moment. On the other hand, according to the New Testament revelation, our co-resurrection with Christ is also an accomplished fact (Eph. 2:6a). We were crucified together with Christ, and we were also resurrected together with Christ. Hence, to be resurrected together with Christ should also be our experience every moment (Phil. 3:10a). It is through this experience of resurrection that we can be conformed to His death.

Taking Life and the Body as the Principle

The fourth aspect of the living of the Body of Christ is that of taking life and the Body as the principle. We have already mentioned that in the living of every kind of life there is its definite regulation and principle. The principle of the living of the Body of Christ is nothing other than life and the Body. To take life as the principle is to take the intrinsic life of God, which is Christ as the embodiment of God (1 John 5:11-12), and not man's outward conduct and morality (Rom. 9:11b; Gal. 2:16a), as the principle. You should never have the thought that since now you are saved and are a Christian, you should take good conduct and a good moral standard as your principle. It should not be like that. That is not the living that the Body of Christ should have; that is just a living according to human goodness. We Christians are regenerated in our spirit; thus, we have life, not morality, as the principle. We have to live Christ out, not morality. Our taking Christ as life as the principle of our living should be with gentleness, politeness, honor to our parents, humility, and patience; yet all these should be the living out of Christ from within us by the Spirit, and not something worked out by our own striving and effort. Therefore, we love Christ and draw near to Christ. The Spirit of Christ fills us within so that from within us Christ may be lived out as all these virtues. Honoring others is Christ; love is Christ; forbearing is Christ; humility and patience are also Christ. All our virtues are the living out of Christ from our spirit.

Furthermore, our living also takes the Body as its principle. We all are the members of the Body of Christ. Each member lives Christ out by the Spirit of life (Phil. 1:19-21a). At the same time, we live corporately, not individualistically. Whether the living of an individual member is good or bad relates just to that member himself, not the Body. Only by a corporate living and a living out of Christ in coordination will we have the living of the Body of Christ, which will be the fullness of Christ for expressing Him (Rom. 12:5; Eph. 1:23). Therefore, our normal living should have the consciousness of the Body of Christ. Any living that is not joined to the Body of Christ does not have the consciousness of the Body of Christ. We should accept the regulation of the Body of Christ in order to live out the life that has the Body of Christ as the principle.

(A message given by Brother Witness Lee on April 14, 1990, in Taipei, Taiwan.)

CHAPTER FOUR

THE SERVICE OF THE BODY OF CHRIST

Scripture Reading: Rom. 12:1, 5; 1 Pet. 2:5, 9; Rom. 15:16;
Eph. 4:11-12; Acts 2:36; 2 Cor. 4:5a; Acts 13:2; 1:8; Matt.
28:18-19; Acts 4:31b; 1 Cor. 2:4; Acts 6:10; 11:18; Rom. 12:4;
1 Cor. 12:7, 11; John 21:15-17; 1 Cor. 14:1, 3-5, 12, 24, 31; Eph.
4:16; 1 Pet. 2:2; Col. 1:28-29

OUTLINE

I. Being the service of the New Testament priesthood of
the gospel—1 Pet. 2:5, 9:
  A. Being centered on the preaching of the gospel to
  save sinners and offer them as sacrifices to
  God—Rom. 15:16.
  B. The goal being to build up the Body of Christ—
  Eph. 4:11-12.
II. Taking Christ as the Lord—Acts 2:36; 2 Cor. 4:5a;
Acts 13:2:
  A. According to Christ's heart's desire.
  B. For Christ's purpose.
III. Taking the Holy Spirit as power and authority—Acts
1:8; Matt. 28:18-19:
  A. Preaching the Word of God by the power of the
  Spirit—Acts 4:31b; 1 Cor. 2:4; Acts 6:10.
  B. Dispensing life by the Spirit—Acts 11:18.
IV. Taking the Body as the means—Rom. 12:5:
  A. Every member participating in service—Rom.
  12:4; 1 Cor. 12:7, 11.
  B. Being the corporate service of the Body in the
  coordination of the Body—Rom. 12:5:

      1. Preaching the gospel to save sinners—Rom. 15:16.

      2. Feeding the Lord's lambs and shepherding the Lord's flock—John 21:15-17.

      3. Perfecting the saints to build up the Body of Christ—Eph. 4:11-12.

      4. Prophesying, speaking for the Lord, to build up the church—1 Cor. 14:1, 3-5, 12, 24, 31.

  C. The Body building itself up through every joint of the supply and through every functioning member—Eph. 4:16.

V. The three steps of offering by the priests of the gospel in the Body:

  A. Leading sinners to salvation and offering them as sacrifices to God—1 Pet. 2:9b, 5b; Rom. 15:16.

  B. Nourishing the believers so that they may grow up and present themselves as living sacrifices to God—1 Pet. 2:2; Rom. 12:1.

  C. Laboring and struggling in all wisdom to present every one of the saints full grown in Christ—Col. 1:28-29.

Prayer: O Lord Jesus, we thank and praise You from the depths of our being. You have blessed the previous three meetings, and now You have brought us to this meeting tonight. As You have given us a glorious beginning and a glorious continuation, do grant us a glorious conclusion, so that we may see a blessing from You greater than what we have witnessed on the previous evenings. We pray that You would speak to us again and release to us the wonders in Your Word. Cleanse us with Your blood and anoint us with Your holy ointment. Anoint the speaker as well as the hearers. Anoint every one in this meeting so that we may all receive a supply from You. Lord Jesus, glorify Yourself and sanctify Your holy name. Lord, we exalt You, we worship You, and we joyfully praise You. Amen.

THE SERVICE OF THE BODY OF CHRIST BEING ORGANIC AS WELL AS PARTICULAR

This is the last meeting. In the previous three meetings, we saw the origin of the Body of Christ, the elements, essence, and reality of the Body of Christ, and the living of the Body of Christ. Now we want to consider the service of the Body of Christ. The Body of Christ is an organism with its origin, its constituents, its elements, the essence in its constituents, and its reality which is manifested without. All these things spontaneously produce a certain kind of living.

In the previous message, we said that the living of the Body of Christ takes Christ as the Head, the life, and the center, and the Spirit as the essence and the reality, the crucifixion and resurrection of Christ as the rule, and life and the Body as the principle. I believe that we have all seen this and have received an amount of help from it. We now come to see the service of the Body of Christ. Although the word *service* is common, it is not a simple matter. According to its proper meaning, it is better to render this word as *ministry*. In common terms, a ministry means a special assignment. This is like a mail carrier who has been particularly sent to accomplish a special goal.

Although outstanding results are yet to be seen after four or five years of struggling and striving, the practice of the new way is becoming more and more apparent each day. This morning we had a meeting with the new ones who came in through the spread of our gospelization work. Among the two thousand attendants, over thirteen hundred people were saved within the past year in different towns and villages. They are the fruit borne by our gospel teams that have gone out. This work of spreading the gospel in the countryside is truly a special assignment. For the past fifteen months, since January a year ago, our brothers and sisters have gone to the countryside with a commission. They have been farming laboriously by sowing in tears. Now they are bringing in their sheaves with joy.

I sat there watching them meeting and singing. They did not look like new believers, but like professionals who knew how to sing, smile, and express themselves. I was deeply touched by them. I could tell from their testimonies that some were older, and others were younger; some were highly educated, while others were not; some were rough, and others were refined. Such a variety of people was simply too wonderful. This is the fruit of the new way. There was not even a hint of Christianity among them. They were living, organic, spiritual, and full of life. This is why I feel that since the Body of Christ is a living organism, its service must be living and organic. If we as the members of Christ can neither laugh or weep, jump or shout, it is difficult for our service to be effectual. Only when we are living can we serve successfully. When we are solemn and dull, we can only bind and shackle others. In gospel preaching, we ourselves must first be released by the Lord before we can release others.

The service of the Body of Christ is not only living and organic, it is also particular. Even the smallest thing we do in the Body of Christ is particular. Whether preaching the gospel or feeding the lambs, each member must receive a particular burden from the Lord and do his best to fulfill his own service. If a church has many preaching the gospel and shepherding the lambs, if it is full of gospel and shepherding activities, it will surely be prevailing. You all must learn to do the Lord's work by special assignment so that you can fulfill your service in the Body. This does not mean that you must be full-time but that you should contact people spontaneously in your daily life. You can preach the gospel to your classmates while playing ball with them, and you can feed the lambs over the telephone. In any event, we all must serve in the Body of Christ, and we must do so in a particular way.

THE SERVICE OF THE BODY OF CHRIST

Being the Service of the New Testament Priesthood of the Gospel

The service of the church as the Body of Christ is the service of the New Testament priesthood of the gospel (1 Pet. 2:5, 9). It is the service of the New Testament, and it is of the gospel and of a priesthood. A priest is individualistic, whereas a priesthood is corporate. It is much like a ball team which is a corporate entity. A ball game is not played by any one individual, but by a group. Our service must also be carried out as a corporate entity, the New Testament priesthood of the gospel. The foremost thing of this service is to center on the preaching of the gospel to save sinners and to offer them as sacrifices to God (Rom. 15:16). In a general sense, gospel preaching is soul-winning. This is not wrong, but such a goal is not high enough. Our emphasis in gospel preaching is not on this but on God receiving an offering. According to the revelation of the Old Testament, our God daily anticipates our offering to Him. Actually, the offering of sacrifices must be done not only daily but also every morning and evening.

Our gospel preaching today is not merely to win souls but to save sinners one by one and offer them as sacrifices to God. This is the focus of our service. When I was first saved, I heard that I must preach the gospel diligently to save souls. Later, I also heard that I must preach the gospel diligently in order to bear fruit. Fruit-bearing seems a little higher than soul-winning. In the last two years, I began to realize that we are God's priests and that our gospel preaching cannot merely be soul-winning or fruit-bearing. It is to save the sinners and offer them to God as sacrifices. Suppose you preach the gospel to someone and baptize him after he believes and receives. Now you must remember to offer this person as a sacrifice to God in your prayers. If you do this, you will be a joyful person. This is the focus of our service as the New Testament priests of the gospel.

Furthermore, the service of the New Testament priesthood of the gospel has as its goal the building up of the Body of Christ (Eph. 4:11-12). The focus of our service is to save sinners and offer them to God, while the goal is to build up the Body of Christ. After we preach the gospel, lead a sinner to salvation, and offer him as a sacrifice to God, that sacrifice becomes material for the building up of the Body of Christ. In returning to Taipei this time, I am very happy to see that you have gone on in the new way. Although the speed of advancement is not that great, you are nevertheless progressing in a solid way. I am especially delighted to see so many new ones brought in through the spread of our gospelization work. They are being offered to God as sacrifices, and they have all become materials for the building up of the Body of Christ. Without materials, it is vain to talk about building. Now we have so much material for the building up of Christ's Body. This is the result of the new way.

Taking Christ as the Lord

Furthermore, we must take Christ as Lord in the service of the Body of Christ and of the church (Acts 2:36; 2 Cor. 4:5a; Acts 13:2). This is according to Christ's desire and for Christ's purpose. We must not take any person as Lord except Christ. When we serve in the Body of Christ, we must learn to seek the Lord much in all things through prayer, and ask Him to lead us in order that we may know His heart's desire and understand His purpose. Only He is the Lord. Though we do not see Him, He is still the Lord, and though we cannot touch Him, He is present with us. Through Him, we can deal with and be brought through all the hindrances and problems that we encounter in our service. Thus, we must learn to acknowledge Him as Lord, to fellowship with Him constantly, to seek His presence, and to know His heart's desire and His purpose.

Taking the Holy Spirit as Power and Authority

In the service of the Body of Christ we not only take Christ as Lord but also take the Holy Spirit as power and authority (Acts 1:8; Matt. 28:18-19). To do anything we need power and authority. The Holy Spirit is our power and authority in the service of the Body of Christ. The Lord said in Matthew 28:18-19, "All authority has been given to Me in heaven and on earth. Go therefore and disciple all the nations." When the Lord spoke this word, He had already given us all power and authority. Thus, we must consider it a fact that the Christ who was transfigured as the Holy Spirit is with us when we go to preach the gospel. The Holy Spirit who is present with us is our power and authority.

There may be times when you preach the gospel to a stubborn and unyielding person. You should pray in your heart, "Lord, Your authority is here. Exercise Your authority over this one." When you apply the authority which the Lord has given to you in this way, quite often you will witness people being softened to such an extent that they eventually receive the Lord into their hearts, call upon the Lord's name, and get baptized. Therefore, learn to preach the Word of God by the power of the Holy Spirit (Acts 4:31b; 1 Cor. 2:4; Acts 6:10) and to dispense life by the Holy Spirit (Acts 11:18). The Holy Spirit is present with you. Do not speak by the natural man outwardly, but rather speak by an inward exercise of the power and authority given by the Holy Spirit.

Taking the Body as the Means

Every Member Serving
in the Coordination of the Body

Furthermore, we also need to take the Body as our means (Rom. 12:5). This Body is not our body, but Christ's. When you go to preach the gospel, the entire Body is going, not you alone. You are preaching in the Body and serving in the Body. We are the Body of Christ, and in this Body every member serves (Rom. 12:4; 1 Cor. 12:7, 11). Moreover, each one serves in the coordination of the Body, resulting in a corporate service of the Body (Rom. 12:5). In preaching the gospel, it is best that three or five join together, with some of them going out to preach, others praying at home, and all having fellowship together afterwards. This is coordination.

The big gospel meetings of the past were good except for one shortcoming: only one spoke and not all could function. Suppose everyone here in the audience would go and contact people for gospel preaching by either visiting, making phone calls, or writing gospel letters. I believe the result of all this would be much greater than that of one man speaking every day. I realize that you are often occupied, but still you can do this kind of work once a week. You can make telephone calls. Try to get some telephone numbers. You can begin by calling up your relatives, acquaintances, colleagues, or classmates and talking with them on the phone. You can also make an appointment to visit them or write a gospel letter to them. I absolutely believe that if you would do these three things together—letter writing, telephoning, and visiting—in the coordination of the Body, they will be very effective.

In most big corporations today, tasks are spread out among many people and not concentrated in the hands of a few. Our mistake in the old way was due to the principle of being dependent on one or two persons to do everything. Modern business administration seeks to abandon this principle in favor of division of labor and mutual cooperation. This is also the principle of our practice of the new way—everyone should be involved. The clearest example of this is that two thousand new fruit have been brought in during the past year or so by two hundred people who went to the countryside to spread the gospel. Surely we would not have gained this fruit if these two hundred had not gone out. In the same respect, would we not have gained still more if we had sent out more? If we had relied only on a few speakers, the number we would gain in a few years would probably be quite small.

For this reason, I want to share with you one thing which can be easily achieved. I hope that after their graduation from college, our young people would not be anxious to further their education or to find jobs immediately. Rather, they should set apart two years of their time for church service by serving the Lord on a full-time basis. They should spend a year in the training and another year in the villages. After two years, they can then consider how the Lord would lead them—to serve the Lord full-time for the rest of their lives or to serve the Lord with a job like most others. By this way, there will be a rotation of serving ones among us to bring the gospel to all of Taiwan.

We have not fully preached the gospel even in Taipei. The total number of saved people in Taiwan does not amount to five percent of its total population. If the college graduates among us would be led to serve the church for two years upon graduation by preaching the gospel in a persistent, steady, and diligent way through phone calls, gospel letters, or visitations, and if they would be coordinated with all the saints in the corporate service of the Body, I do believe the church will experience a great increase.

I have been taking the lead in the practice of the new way here for more than five years. There are still three things that I would like to do which have not been done. First, the majority of the eighty or more elders in the twenty-three halls in Taipei are young people. All these elders need shepherding. Yet we have not had the appropriate persons to shepherd them in the past few years. Second, in the past practice of the new way we have stressed only door-to-door visitation for gospel preaching and not telephoning or letter writing. From now on, we must do all three. At the same time, we need to hold "reaping" meetings at least once a month, so that our gospel can be preached more thoroughly and completely. We should bring our contacts from our districts, groups, and homes together to hear the preaching of the truths of the gospel by the gifted ones that they may be reaped. Third, we do not yet have an adequate meeting hall to accommodate the increase of believers among us. I anticipate that in the near future we will be able to build a meeting hall that can seat ten thousand people on our property on Hsin-Yi Road. Then we can have conferences every two or three months to release the Lord's messages. This is also a great need. Do pray much for the ongoing developments concerning the building up of that hall.

Being the Corporate Service of the Body

The corporate service of the whole Body is the scriptural way. It causes every member to fulfill his or her organic function in the Body. There are four main items in such a service. First, we must preach the gospel to save sinners (Rom. 15:16). We must continually bring the gospel to people to lead them to salvation, either by visiting them by knocking on their doors, calling them on the phone, or writing them letters. Second, we must feed the Lord's lambs and shepherd His flock (John 21:15-17). Third, we must perfect the saints to build up the Body of Christ (Eph. 4:11-12). This matter is not found in Christianity, and yet it is revealed in the Scriptures. It is the Lord's mercy that we have adopted it as part of the Lord's recovery. The gifted ones should not be the only ones who perfect the saints; the saints themselves should become gifted ones to perfect others. Fourth, every saint can prophesy and speak for the Lord to build up the church, the Body of Christ (1 Cor. 14:1, 3-5, 12, 24, 31).

The Body Building Itself Up through Every Joint of the Supply and through Every Functioning Member

The Body of Christ builds itself up through every joint of the supply and through every functioning member (Eph. 4:16). There are two kinds of members in the Body, the supplying joints and the operating parts. The operation of our physical body depends on the joints. In the Body of Christ, we also need some who can be joints for the purpose of supplying others. The supply stations of the blood are the joints in the body. Without the joints, the Body cannot receive the supply. In addition to the joints, there is the need for another group of members, such as the hands and fingers, with their own particular functions. With the joints of supply and every functioning part, the Body can now build itself up in love. Our physical body builds itself up. If we do not eat, we are unable to build up our body. This is the same with the church. We all are members. But some are joints supplying, while the other parts are being active in fulfilling their function as members. In this way, the Body will build itself up.

The Three Steps of Offering by the Priests of the Gospel in the Service of the Body

Finally, we have to mention the three steps of offering by the priests of the gospel in the Body service. The first step is to lead sinners to salvation and to offer them as sacrifices to God (1 Pet. 2:9b, 5b; Rom. 15:16). Next we have to nourish them so that they may grow up and present themselves as living sacrifices to God (1 Pet. 2:2; Rom. 12:1). Initially, they were saved and offered to God, but now, as they have grown up, they offer themselves to God. Lastly, the gifted ones still need to labor and struggle in all wisdom to present every saint full-grown in Christ to God (Col. 1:28-29). At this point, the saints will have become full-grown in the stature of Christ, and the Body of Christ can be fully built.

I hope that after these four meetings the church here has seen something and that the brothers and sisters know the origin of the Body of Christ as well as its elements, essence, and reality. I hope that they will have the living of the Body of Christ and the service of the Body of Christ to fulfill their function in the Body service. Then the Lord will have a way among us. May the Lord give grace to each of you, and may each one of you receive these words and practice them diligently by His grace.

(A message given by Brother Witness Lee on April 15, 1990, in Taipei, Taiwan.)

ABOUT THE AUTHOR

Witness Lee was born in 1905 in northern China and raised in a Christian family. At age 19 he was fully captured for Christ and immediately consecrated himself to preach the gospel for the rest of his life. Early in his service, he met Watchman Nee, a renowned preacher, teacher, and writer. Witness Lee labored together with Watchman Nee under his direction. In 1934 Watchman Nee entrusted Witness Lee with the responsibility for his publication operation, called the Shanghai Gospel Bookroom.

Prior to the Communist takeover in 1949, Witness Lee was sent by Watchman Nee and his other co-workers to Taiwan to ensure that the things delivered to them by the Lord would not be lost. Watchman Nee instructed Witness Lee to continue the former's publishing operation abroad as the Taiwan Gospel Bookroom, which has been publicly recognized as the publisher of Watchman Nee's works outside China. Witness Lee's work in Taiwan manifested the Lord's abundant blessing. From a mere 350 believers, newly fled from the mainland, the churches in Taiwan grew to 20,000 in five years.

In 1962 Witness Lee felt led of the Lord to come to the United States, settling in California. During his 35 years of service in the U.S., he ministered in weekly meetings and weekend conferences, delivering several thousand spoken messages. Much of his speaking has since been published as over 400 titles. Many of these have been translated into over fourteen languages. He gave his last public conference in February 1997 at the age of 91.

He leaves behind a prolific presentation of the truth in the Bible. His major work, *Life-study of the Bible*, comprises over 25,000 pages of commentary on every book of the Bible from the perspective of the believers' enjoyment and experience of God's divine life in Christ through the Holy Spirit. Witness Lee was the chief editor of a new translation of the New Testament into Chinese called the Recovery Version and directed the translation of the same into English. The Recovery Version also appears in a number of other languages. He provided an extensive body of footnotes, outlines, and spiritual cross references. A radio broadcast of his messages can be heard on Christian radio stations in the United States. In 1965 Witness Lee founded Living Stream Ministry, a non-profit corporation, located in Anaheim, California, which officially presents his and Watchman Nee's ministry.

Witness Lee's ministry emphasizes the experience of Christ as life and the practical oneness of the believers as the Body of Christ. Stressing the importance of attending to both these matters, he led the churches under his care to grow in Christian life and function. He was unbending in his conviction that God's goal is not narrow sectarianism but the Body of Christ. In time, believers began to meet simply as the church in their localities in response to this conviction. In recent years a number of new churches have been raised up in Russia and in many eastern European countries.